READY FOR MILITARY ACTION

REMARKABLE
MILITARY ANIMALS

by Carla Mooney

Content Consultant
Mitchell A. Yockelson
Adjunct Faculty
US Naval Academy

Core Library

An Imprint of Abdo Publishing
www.abdopublishing.com

www.abdopublishing.com

Published by Abdo Publishing, a division of ABDO, PO Box 398166, Minneapolis, Minnesota 55439. Copyright © 2015 by Abdo Consulting Group, Inc. International copyrights reserved in all countries. No part of this book may be reproduced in any form without written permission from the publisher. Core Library™ is a trademark and logo of Abdo Publishing.

Printed in the United States of America, North Mankato, Minnesota
092014
012015

THIS BOOK CONTAINS
RECYCLED MATERIALS

Cover Photo: Photographers Mate 1st Class Brien Aho/US Department of Defense
Interior Photos: Photographers Mate 1st Class Brien Aho/US Department of Defense, 1, 36; Maranda Flynn/US Department of Defense, 4; Staff Sgt. Matthew T MacRoberts/US Department of Defense, 7; K9 Storm Incorporated, 8; Stephen Dalton/NHPA/Photoshot/ Newscom, 10; Shutterstock Images, 12, 19; Dorling Kindersley/Thinkstock, 14; Bettmann/ Corbis, 17; David Kay/Shutterstock Images, 20; Lance Cpl. Ali Azimi/US Department of Defense, 22; Alex Sgt. Jose A. Torres Jr/US Department of Defense, 26; Spc. Daniel Bearl/ US Department of Defense, 28; Spc. Adrianna Lucas and Pvt. Chae, Ki-soo/US Department of Defense, 31, 45; Illustrator Draftsman 1st Class Pierre G. Georges/US Department of Defense, 34; Thinkstock, 38; Mass Communication Specialist 2nd Class Jennifer A. Villalovos/ US Department of Defense, 40; US Department of Defense, 42; KRT/Newscom, 43

Editor: Patrick Donnelly
Series Designer: Becky Daum

Library of Congress Control Number: 2014944233

Cataloging-in-Publication Data
Mooney, Carla.
 Remarkable military animals / Carla Mooney.
  p. cm. -- (Ready for military action)
ISBN 978-1-62403-655-2 (lib. bdg.)
Includes bibliographical references and index.
1. Animals--War use--Juvenile literature. 2. Animals in police work--Juvenile literature.   I. Title.
355.4--dc23
                                                                        2014944233

CONTENTS

CHAPTER ONE

HUNTING TERRORISTS

On the night of May 1, 2011, 23 US Navy SEALs, a Pakistani-American translator, and a dog boarded two Blackhawk helicopters. The stealth aircraft left Jalalabad Airfield in eastern Afghanistan. The elite soldiers flew through the night sky, making their way to Pakistan.

The SEALs were on a top secret mission. The Central Intelligence Agency (CIA) believed that

The Belgian Malinois is an intelligent and fearless breed of dog.

Bomb-Sniffing Bees

Bees are insects with a surprising military purpose. Scientists are working to train honeybees to detect bombs. Bees have a fantastic sense of smell. Scientists are training the bees to find explosives by rewarding them with sugar water. If trained successfully, bees could be used to find mines. Bees cost less than bomb-sniffing dogs. They are also small enough to not set off the mines.

the terrorist leader Osama bin Laden was hiding in a house in Abbottabad, Pakistan. On September 11, 2001, al-Qaeda terrorists hijacked airplanes and crashed them into the World Trade Center skyscrapers in New York City and the Pentagon, the US military headquarters in Washington, DC. Another hijacked plane crashed near Shanksville, Pennsylvania. Almost 3,000 people were killed in the attacks. As the leader of al-Qaeda, bin Laden was responsible for the attacks. The SEALs' mission was to find bin Laden and capture or kill him.

One helicopter carried Cairo, a highly trained military working dog. Cairo was a Belgian Malinois.

Military dogs like Cairo can be fitted with harnesses that allow them to be lowered from aircraft to the ground.

A Malinois is a lot like a German shepherd, but slightly smaller. They usually weigh about 55 to 65 pounds (25 to 29.5 kg).

Cairo's Mission

Like the other members of the SEAL team, Cairo had been on many missions. He could sniff a piece of clothing and find the person to whom it belonged. Cairo could find someone who was hiding and

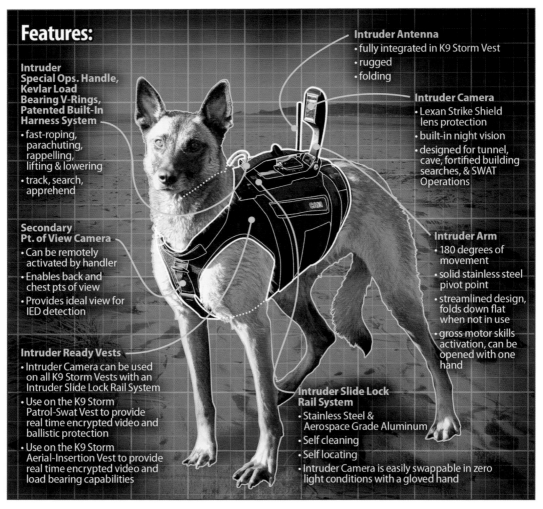

Features:

Intruder Antenna
- fully integrated in K9 Storm Vest
- rugged
- folding

Intruder Special Ops. Handle, Kevlar Load Bearing V-Rings, Patented Built-In Harness System
- fast-roping, parachuting, rappelling, lifting & lowering
- track, search, apprehend

Intruder Camera
- Lexan Strike Shield lens protection
- built-in night vision
- designed for tunnel, cave, fortified building searches, & SWAT Operations

Secondary Pt. of View Camera
- Can be remotely activated by handler
- Enables back and chest pts of view
- Provides ideal view for IED detection

Intruder Arm
- 180 degrees of movement
- solid stainless steel pivot point
- streamlined design, folds down flat when not in use
- gross motor skills activation, can be opened with one hand

Intruder Ready Vests
- Intruder Camera can be used on all K9 Storm Vests with an Intruder Slide Lock Rail System
- Use on the K9 Storm Patrol-Swat Vest to provide real time encrypted video and ballistic protection
- Use on the K9 Storm Aerial-Insertion Vest to provide real time encrypted video and load bearing capabilities

Intruder Slide Lock Rail System
- Stainless Steel & Aerospace Grade Aluminum
- Self cleaning
- Self locating
- Intruder Camera is easily swappable in zero light conditions with a gloved hand

K9 Storm Intruder

Military dogs like Cairo often wear specially designed body armor during a mission. How does this armor protect a dog? How does it assist during a mission?

signal whether the person was dead or alive. Cairo also sniffed out explosives, trip wires, and other booby traps.

After 90 minutes in the air, the Blackhawks reached their target. They descended toward the compound. Cairo's copter landed on the lawn. Cairo and the SEALs leapt into action.

On the Move

As some of the SEALs stormed the building, Cairo took his position outside. His job was to help secure the perimeter of the bin Laden house. He also searched for bombs. If needed, Cairo was prepared to attack the enemy. He wore a specially designed vest made of a protective material called Kevlar. It had harnesses for parachuting and

Glowworms

Animals have been used in military operations for a long time. In World War I (1914–1918) soldiers used the European glowworm to light the cold, dark trenches. The men gathered the glowworms and put them in jars. Just 10 glowworms could give the same amount of light as a modern streetlight. Using the glowworms' light, soldiers were able to read intelligence reports and study battle maps. They could also read letters from home.

Glowworms like this one were used during World War I to provide light in the trenches.

rappelling, or climbing down a steep surface on a rope. It also had a night-vision camera.

Minutes later, word came from inside the house. The SEALs had found and killed bin Laden. Forty minutes after arriving, Cairo and his SEAL team flew back to Afghanistan, carrying bin Laden's body. The mission was a success.

Animals like Cairo are valuable members of the US military. Today's military uses animals for a wide variety of jobs from bomb-sniffing to patrolling the country's coastline. These animals use their unique abilities to protect and help US soldiers and sailors.

In this passage from *Trident K9 Warriors*, author Mike Ritland, a military dog handler, writes about the traits of a good military dog:

> The military working dogs that accompany the Navy SEALs are not like the average pet in several ways. Though human aggression components [are] probably the most obvious, there are other ways in which these dogs are not your typical house pet, no matter how well-bred those dogs might be. These dogs are also highly motivated and extremely energetic. One way to put this into context is for you to think of the most ball-crazy dog you've ever seen. You know the type—the one who will pursue a ball faster, for greater amounts of time, and with a maniacal determination that has you shaking your head or getting rotator-cuff surgery after throwing or flinging a ball for too many hours a day to satisfy its craving.

Source: Mike Ritland and Gary Brozek. Trident K9 Warriors. New York: St. Martin's Press, 2013. Print. 28.

Back It Up

The author of this passage is using evidence to support a point. Write a paragraph describing the point the author is making. Then write down two or three pieces of evidence the author uses to make the point.

CHAPTER TWO

ANIMALS IN WAR

H umans have used animals in the military for thousands of years. These brave animals have fought next to soldiers in battle. They have also given comfort in the trenches. Animals of all kinds have shown loyalty in the most difficult times.

Animals in Ancient Times

Before 1500 BCE the Mesopotamians hitched horses to their chariots during battles. Ancient Egyptian

A cavalry unit in a Civil War (1861–1865) reenactment

Ancient Egyptians often fought their enemies from horse-drawn chariots.

and Chinese soldiers also fought from horse-drawn chariots. Other early armies rode horses into battle. Foot soldiers were driven back by troops charging on horseback. Some troops fired arrows on horseback.

As early as 1700 BCE, ancient armies in India, Asia, and China brought war elephants to battles. The elephants charged and trampled enemy soldiers. They also pierced and threw soldiers with their tusks and trunks. During the 300s BCE Macedonian king Alexander the Great used elephants in battles. Ancient Greeks, Carthaginians, and Romans also used war elephants.

Many ancient armies also brought dogs to the battlefield. Large breeds like the mastiff fought with ancient Egyptians. Ancient Romans armed their dogs with spiked collars and body armor. Spanish troops used armored attack dogs in the 1500s CE in South America. Native Americans also fought with war dogs by their sides.

War Pigs

The Ancient Romans used squealing war pigs to spook enemy soldiers. The pigs also scared enemy elephants and caused them to run. The panicked elephants trampled anything in their path as they fled. Some armies set pigs on fire to get them to squeal. Then soldiers swung the pigs from city walls to scatter approaching enemy elephants.

Animals in the US Military

Since its earliest days, the US military also has used animals. Horses, pigeons, dogs, chickens, dolphins, beluga whales, sea lions, and other animals have been used in combat and other missions. Many of these animals are still used in the modern military.

Horses

During the Revolutionary War (1775–1783) General George Washington created cavalry units called the Continental Dragoons. A cavalry is a unit of soldiers that fight on horseback. In the Civil War (1861–1865) the North and South used cavalry units. Horses were also used in World War I. However, tanks and machine guns replaced many horses on the battlefield. By 1942 the US military had stopped using horses regularly in combat.

Dogs

The US military used dogs throughout the 1800s. These dogs were mostly pets or mascots. They kept the soldiers company and provided comfort and entertainment. But in World War I military dogs showed they could be put to work too.

Stubby, a pit bull mix, was one of the most honored animals in World War I.

In 1917 a stray pit bull mix named Stubby proved he could be valuable during combat. Stubby wandered onto the Yale University campus in Connecticut. Members of the army's 102nd Infantry Regiment were training there. Stubby participated in drills. He even learned how to salute with his right paw. A private adopted Stubby. When the private was sent to the front lines, he smuggled the dog with him.

On the front lines, Stubby learned to warn the men before a poison gas attack by barking and covering his nose with his paws. He found wounded soldiers during patrols. Once, Stubby attacked a German spy and held him until soldiers arrived. This earned Stubby the rank of sergeant. Sergeant Stubby survived 17 battles. After the war, Sergeant Stubby became a national hero. He led parades and received awards until his death in 1926.

By 1942 the military realized the potential of dogs in combat. They trained the dogs for guard and police duty. The dogs tracked enemy soldiers and found and rescued wounded soldiers. Dogs ran messages and laid telegraph lines by carrying wire attached to their collars. They sniffed out land mines. They also patrolled as guard dogs.

Cher Ami

During World War I, a pigeon named Cher Ami flew for the US Army Signal Corps in France. He delivered 12 important messages to the Americans near Verdun, France. On his last mission Cher Ami was shot. Even though he was injured, he delivered his message: the "Lost Battalion" of the US 77th Infantry Division was trapped behind enemy lines. A mission was launched and 194 men were rescued.

Homing pigeons like these have been trained to serve as military messengers since ancient times.

War Pigeons

Not all military animals served on the ground. Ancient Greeks and Persians used homing pigeons as military messengers. They flew high and fast. They also could find their way to specific locations. This allowed them to carry messages for hundreds of miles. During World War I and World War II, the United States and England used special pigeon units to communicate with soldiers on the front lines.

CHAPTER THREE

RIDING HIGH

Horses and mules have been an important part of the military throughout American history. Although their role today is more limited, these animals have served bravely in many wars and missions.

Mules in the Military

A mule is part donkey, part horse. Mules are ideal pack animals. They can carry heavy loads over long

The riderless horse is one of the oldest traditions at military funerals.

The US military uses mules to haul big loads over rough terrain.

distances. A mule can carry as much as 300 pounds (136 kg), seven hours a day, for 20 days in a row. They also eat less than horses and are not injured as often.

From the early 1800s through the 1900s, mules were commonly used by the US Army and other military branches. Pack mules allow the military to move supplies and equipment through all types of terrain. Before the military began using cars and trucks, mules carried or pulled food, weapons, and other supplies. Today, mules still transport supplies through rocky mountains or other areas where vehicles cannot travel.

Horse Soldiers

No animal has a longer history in the US military than the horse. Cavalry horses carried soldiers into battle. Along with mules, horses carried or pulled supplies and equipment needed by armies.

During the Korean War (1950–1953) a pony named Reckless worked with the US Marine 5th Regiment. She navigated the mountainous trails

The Riderless Horse

One of the oldest military traditions in a full honor funeral is the riderless horse. A solider leads the riderless horse behind the caisson. The horse wears an empty saddle. The rider's boots are reversed in the stirrups to show that the soldier will never ride again. Riderless horses have followed the caissons bearing the caskets of presidents Franklin D. Roosevelt, John F. Kennedy, and Dwight D. Eisenhower.

and hills and carried ammunition. During the Battle of Outpost Vegas in March 1953, Reckless hauled ammunition for three days and nights. She had only short breaks for water, food, and rest. She was wounded twice but was bandaged and returned to work. On one day alone Reckless made 51 trips covering more than 35 miles (56 km) to deliver ammunition. She carried more than 9,000 (4,080 kg) pounds of explosives. On her return trips, Reckless carried dead or wounded soldiers on her back. Because of her bravery, many marines survived the battle.

Therapeutic Riding Program

Horses from the US Army Caisson Platoon have another important duty. The Therapeutic Riding Program uses soldiers and horses to help wounded military veterans. They provide physical and emotional therapy to veterans suffering from injuries and post-traumatic stress. Veterans in the program help care for, groom, and ride the horses during weekly lessons. The program creates a strong bond between the wounded veterans, soldiers, and horses.

In 1960 Reckless retired after being promoted to staff sergeant. Today a statue of Reckless stands at the National Museum of the Marine Corps in Virginia.

However, with the invention of tanks and mechanical vehicles, fewer horses were needed on the battlefield. Today the US Army still uses horses for various ceremonies.

Secret Mission—The Horse Soldiers

Horses made a comeback for a modern mission. In 2001 US Army Special Forces troops entered Afghanistan. They arrived a little more than a month after the al-Qaeda terrorist attack in the United States. A small group of special ops soldiers were sent to secure northern Afghanistan against the enemy. The steep mountainous terrain was extremely difficult to travel. So the troops mounted horses and rode into combat. They carried out several missions using horses, much like a cavalry from the past. It was the first time horses were used in combat by US forces since 1942.

The Caisson Platoon performs ceremonial functions at military funerals and parades.

Caisson Platoon

These days horses are mostly used for ceremonial duties. The soldiers and horses of the Caisson Platoon of the 3rd United States Infantry Regiment are known as the Old Guard. They perform an important duty at military funerals. At a funeral, six horses pull a flag-draped casket on a black artillery caisson. The six horses are matched gray or black. They are paired into three teams. All six horses are saddled, but only the horses on the left have mounted riders. The team pulls the fallen soldier to Arlington National Cemetery in Virginia to be buried.

Excerpt of "The Soldier's Kiss" by Henry Chappell (1874–1937):

> Only a dying horse! Pull off the gear,
> And slip the needless bit from frothing jaws,
> Drag it aside there, leave the roadway clear,
> The battery thunders on with scarce a pause.
> Prone by the shell-swept highway there it lies
> With quivering limbs, as fast the life-tide fails,
> Dark films are closing o'er the faithful eyes
> That mutely plead for aid where none avails.
> Onward the battery rolls, but one there speeds
> Heedless of comrade's voice or bursting shell,
> Back to the wounded friend who lonely bleeds
> Beside the stony highway where he fell.
> Only a dying horse! He swiftly kneels,
> Lifts the limp head and hears the shivering sigh
> Kisses his friend, while down his cheek there steals
> Sweet pity's tear: 'Goodbye old man. Goodbye.'

Source: Henry Chappell. "The Soldier's Kiss." Animals in War Memorial. AIW, 2014. Web. Accessed July 29, 2014.

What's the Big Idea?

Reread Chappell's poem carefully. Have a parent or teacher help you understand what it means. What is its main idea? Which details support the main idea? Name two or three details Chappell uses to support his main idea.

CHAPTER FOUR

BOMB-SNIFFING DOGS

Today dogs are the animals most frequently used by the US military. These dogs perform a variety of jobs. There are about 2,800 active-duty US military dogs.

Some of the best breeds for military dogs are the German shepherd and Belgian Malinois. These breeds have excellent noses for detection. The Malinois is lighter and stubbier than the shepherd. Some military

Military dogs often are fitted with special goggles to protect their eyes and help them spot targets.

The Dickin Medal

The Dickin Medal honors the bravest animals in war. The medal is awarded in the United Kingdom to animals of any nation that display courage or devotion to duty. It is the highest award any animal can receive while serving in war. The Dickin Medal was first awarded in 1943. Since then it has been awarded 65 times. It has been given to 32 pigeons, 29 dogs, 3 horses, and 1 cat.

groups train Labrador retrievers because they are hard workers.

The Nose Knows

A dog is one of the best smelling machines in the world. Canine noses have up to 300 million olfactory receptors. These are nerve cells that detect scents. Humans only have about six million. Also, the part of a dog's brain that is used for analyzing smells is about 40 times bigger than that of a human, proportionally. With such a highly developed sense of smell, military dogs are good for detection missions.

A dog's nose is an important tool in its mission. Military dogs use their noses to find improvised explosive devices (IEDs). They search for hidden

This military police dog sniffs for explosive material in a suspicious package.

enemy soldiers. Dogs are also used as combat trackers. They are trained to find and follow the scent of a specific person. Other times dogs patrol as sentries and guards. Once located, the target is unlikely to escape, as the dogs are two times faster than most humans.

Other Skills

On some missions, a dog carrying a video camera will enter a danger zone first. The dog's handlers use the cameras to see what is in the area before the human

Chips

A German shepherd mix named Chips won more medals than any other dog in World War II. Chips served as a guard dog. He traveled throughout Europe, Africa, and Italy with the US Army. In July 1943 Chips saved his handler when Italian soldiers shot at them with a machine gun. Chips rushed at the four shooters and forced them to abandon their cover and surrender to US soldiers. He was wounded during the attack but survived. US Army General Dwight D. Eisenhower personally thanked Chips for his bravery and loyalty.

soldiers follow. Some SEAL dogs parachute jump, in tandem with a handler or solo.

On missions, dogs often wear special strong and flexible body armor to protect against bullets and knife attacks. The armor often carries high-tech equipment. Some dogs wear specially designed goggles that allow the dog to see the heat outline of a human body through a concrete wall.

Military dogs train for missions with a human handler. A strong relationship between the dog and its handler is critical for a successful mission. Handlers know their dogs well. They can spot subtle changes in a dog's behavior that can signal if it has found a dangerous object. When not on active duty, handlers care for their dogs' every need. They feed, clean, and play with them. Handlers are also trained to spot signs of stress in the dogs. Some handlers have become so close to their dogs that they adopt them after the dog retires from the military.

FURTHER EVIDENCE

Chapter Four includes a lot of information about military dogs. If you could pick out the main point of the chapter, what would it be? Find a few pieces of key evidence from the chapter that support the main point. Then explore the website below to learn even more about military dogs. Find a quote from the website that supports the chapter's main point. Does the quote support an existing piece of evidence in the chapter? Or does it add a new piece of evidence? Why?

War Dogs
www.mycorelibrary.com/military-animals

PATROLLING THE SEAS

For more than 40 years, the US Navy Marine Mammal Program has recruited and trained sea creatures for the military. In the early years, navy handlers considered several types of marine mammals for the program. First they attempted to train killer whales and seals for military missions. Eventually bottlenose dolphins and California sea lions became the most successful in the program. These mammals

A navy marine mammal handler demonstrates how dolphins are trained to respond to hand signals.

Sea lions are trained to find mines and identify enemy divers and swimmers.

had excellent underwater senses. They were intelligent and highly trainable. The US Navy used marine mammals for missions in the Vietnam War (1954–1975) and in the first Gulf War (1990–1991). Marine mammals have also been used at several US naval bases.

Marine mammals have an incredible ability to detect and find targets in deep or murky waters.

California sea lions and bottlenose dolphins are hardy and smart. These skills make them very valuable to the military.

The US Navy trains dolphins to detect underwater sea mines. Underwater sea mines are deadly explosive weapons that work in the ocean. A sea mine can sink ships, destroy landing craft, and kill or injure humans. Sea mines can be buried in the seafloor or float from an anchor.

Marine Detectives

Dolphins use sonar to find mines. They send out a series of clicking sounds that bounce off objects in the

Underwater Spies

Scientists at Boston University are working to create remote-control sharks that could become underwater spies. The scientists put thin electrodes into the brains of a dogfish. A dogfish is a member of the shark family. Then scientists use an electrical current to stimulate the shark's sense of smell. The scientist can direct the shark using the generated smell. Using this technology, the military may one day be able to send sharks carrying underwater cameras into the sea as underwater spies.

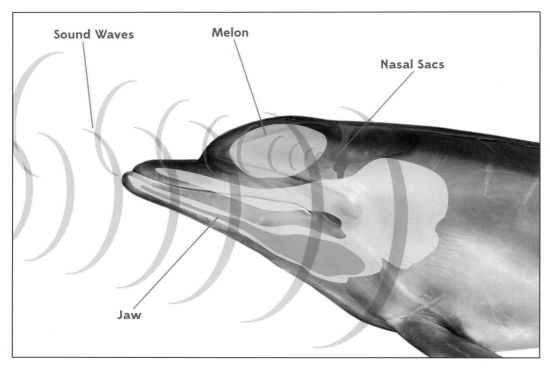

Sound Waves

Melon

Nasal Sacs

Jaw

Echolocation

A dolphin uses echolocation to determine the size and shapes of objects. It uses its nasal sacs to make a click. The click goes through its forehead, or melon, which focuses the sound into a beam. When the beam hits an object, it bounces back to the dolphin. The dolphin's jaw absorbs the returning sound and sends it to the inner ear. The ear and brain interpret the object's size and shape and what it's made of.

area. The dolphins pick up the return echoes and use them to form a mental picture of the area. This ability is called echolocation. The dolphin reports what it finds to its handler through signals that indicate yes or no. If the dolphin finds a mine, the handler can send the dolphin to mark the object's location with a weighted buoy line. Navy dolphins helped detect mines in both Gulf Wars. Navy dolphins can also detect and tag enemy swimmers with a marker so that sailors can catch the swimmers as they attempt to spy or plant explosives.

Sea lions are amphibious. That means they can work in the water and on land. California sea lions have excellent low-light vision and underwater hearing. They can swim up to 25 miles per hour (40 km/h). Sea lions will dive repeatedly up to

Dolphin Demonstration

In 2011 the US Navy showed how its team of sea lions and dolphins protect Americans. In a demonstration a former US Navy SEAL tried to swim undetected into a bay. The SEAL carried an unarmed mine. The navy sent its dolphins and sea lions to patrol the bay. The animals caught the diver on each of his five tries to slip into the harbor. The sea lion attached a clamp to the diver's leg. Navy handlers on the surface reeled the diver in and "captured" him.

US Navy handlers train dolphins to find underwater sea mines.

1,000 feet (300 m). The US Navy uses the sea lions to find and retrieve lost equipment. They are also trained to locate and mark sea mines by attaching grabber devices. If sea lions detect an enemy diver or swimmer, they are trained to attach a special leg cuff to the intruder. Then navy handlers pull the intruder to the surface. Navy sea lions can wear a special harness that carries underwater cameras. As the sea lion swims, the camera sends back live underwater video to navy personnel.

From cavalry horses to patrolling dolphins, many animals have bravely helped the soldiers and sailors of the US military. These animals have shown courage in action and have become valued members of the military team.

EXPLORE ONLINE

Chapter Five discusses the use of marine mammals by the US Navy. The website further explores the US Navy Marine Mammal Program. As you know, every source is different. What facts does the website give about the Marine Mammal Program? How is the information from the website the same as the information in Chapter Five? What new information did you learn from the website?

Marine Mammal Program
www.mycorelibrary.com/military-animals

GI Joe sports his Dickin Medal.

GI Joe Saves Allied Soldiers

On October 18, 1943, a US Army division was supposed to bomb German troops in Colvi Vecchia, Italy. But the Germans retreated unexpectedly. However, British troops had moved into the town shortly before the bombing was to take place. The British soldiers were not able to radio the US troops to cancel the bombing. Desperate, they sent a pigeon named GI Joe with the message to stop the bombing. GI Joe flew 20 miles (32 km) in 20 minutes. He arrived just as the bombers were about to take off. He successfully delivered the message just in time, and the bombing was canceled. GI Joe is credited with saving the lives of more than 100 soldiers that day. He was awarded the Dickin Medal. He was the only American pigeon to receive the honor.

Appollo's Rescue Mission

Although Appollo did not serve in a war, the German shepherd was a hero. He worked as part of the rescue and recovery team after the 2001 terrorist attacks in New York City. Appollo was a member of the K-9 unit of the New York City Police Department. He arrived at the World Trade Center with his handler about 15 minutes after the attack. He was the first search-and-rescue dog at the site after the collapse of the World Trade Center towers. Appollo received the Dickin Medal on behalf of all the dogs involved in the rescue operation.

Appollo with his handler after receiving the Dickin Medal

Navy Dolphins Clear Umm Qasr

In March 2003 dolphins in the US Navy's Special Clearance Team One took part in a mine-clearing operation near Iraq. The dolphins worked with US Navy SEALs, Marine Corps swimmers, explosive weapon disposal divers, and unmanned undersea vehicles. They helped locate and disarm more than 100 antiship mines and underwater booby traps in the port of Umm Qasr in southern Iraq.

STOP AND THINK

Why Do I Care?

This book discusses the different animals used by the US military. Think about two or three ways that working animals connect to your own life. Give examples of parts of your life that have a connection to working animals.

Tell the Tale

Chapter Five discusses the use of marine mammals by the US Navy. Write 200 words that tell the story of a marine mammal's mission. Describe the sights and sounds of the mission. What is the animal looking out for? Be sure to set the scene, develop a sequence of events, and offer a conclusion.

Say What?

Find five words in this book that you have never seen or heard before. Find each word in a dictionary and read the definition. Rewrite the word's definition in your own words. Then use each word in a sentence.

Surprise Me

Reading about military animals can be interesting and surprising. Think about what you learned from this book. Can you name the two or three facts in this book that you found most surprising? Write a short paragraph about each, describing what you found surprising and why.

GLOSSARY

caisson
a two-wheeled vehicle drawn by a horse

cavalry
a unit of soldiers who fight on horseback

handler
a person who trains and directs a military animal

mines
bombs placed underground or underwater

mission
a special job or task for a military soldier or group

olfactory
relating to the sense of smell

outpost
a military base set up far away from the main group of soldiers

post-traumatic
after suffering severe stress or a physical injury

sentries
soldiers or military animals that stand guard and warn others of danger

terrain
ground or land

LEARN MORE

Books

Bausum, Ann. *Stubby the War Dog: The True Story of World War I's Bravest Dog*. Washington, DC: National Geographic, 2014.

Dunn, Joeming. *Cher Ami: WWI Homing Pigeon*. Edina, MN: Magic Wagon, 2012.

Websites

To learn more about the US military and its resources, visit **booklinks.abdopublishing.com**. These links are routinely monitored and updated to provide the most current information available.

Visit **www.mycorelibrary.com** for free additional tools for teachers and students.

INDEX

ABOUT THE AUTHOR

Carla Mooney is the author of several books for young readers. She loves investigating and learning about people, places, and events in history. A graduate of the University of Pennsylvania, she lives in Pittsburgh, Pennsylvania.